© **Standing Tall In Life**
BY SANDEEP RAVIDUTT SHARMA

Table of Contents

Foreword IV

Standing Tall In Life..1

© **Standing Tall In Life**
BY SANDEEP RAVIDUTT SHARMA

Foreword

This book provides you with a list of **100** motivational quotes and thoughts about LIFE, written with the consciousness, grace and energy of **Shiva Shakti**. I'm sure if you keep reading, referring, sharing these thoughts and quotes about LIFE, you may derive inspiration, develop positive outlook and good understanding of various perspectives about life. It needs sincere efforts, discipline and determination to create a unique place for you in this world. There is no shortcut to Success but most of the time a long road which tests you at every corner. The lessons learnt all along the path one day takes you to the *Summit of LIFE* where you stand taller than others.

"Always remember the ground no matter where you stand taller today. It's the first step of your journey that took you to the peak."

I sincerely hope, you will find this book amazing, interesting, rejuvenating, unique and a constant source of inspiration.

Thank You and Happy Reading.

© **Standing Tall In Life**
BY SANDEEP RAVIDUTT SHARMA

Dedication

This book is dedicated to **Shiva Shakti** - the epitome of love. Lord Shiva is pure consciousness symbolising the masculine principle. Goddess Shakti symbolises the active feminine energy of Shiva and is synonymously identified with Tripura Sundari, Sati or Parvati.
These primal principles are also called as Purusha representing consciousness and Prakriti denoting the nature. **Shiva** and **Shakti** are manifestations of the all-in-one divine consciousness. Shiva is the paternal love of God that gives us consciousness, knowledge and clarity. Shakti is the motherly love of God that showers warmth, care and ensures our protection. Shiva and Shakti exist within each of us as the masculine and feminine energy. To please Shiva Shakti praying for the well being, love, happiness, strength, positive energy and success of my readers in their life, I hereby recite the following mantra...

"Sarva Mangala Mangalye Shive Sarvartha Sadhike Sharanye Tryambake Gauri Narayani Namostute"

© Standing Tall In Life
BY SANDEEP RAVIDUTT SHARMA

© **Copyright 2018 Sandeep Ravidutt Sharma - All rights reserved.**
In no way is it legal to reproduce, duplicate, or transmit any part of this document in either electronic means or in printed format. Recording of this publication is strictly prohibited and any storage of this document is not allowed unless with written permission from the publisher. All rights reserved. The information provided herein is stated to be truthful and consistent, in that any liability, in terms of inattention or otherwise, by any usage or abuse of any policies, processes, or directions contained within is the solitary and utter responsibility of the recipient reader. Under no circumstances will any legal responsibility or blame be held against the author / publisher for any reparation, damages, or monetary loss due to the information herein, either directly or indirectly. The author own all copyrights.

Legal Notice:
This book is copyright protected. This is only for personal use. You cannot amend, distribute, sell, use, quote or paraphrase any part or the content within this book without the consent of the author or copyright owner. Legal action will be pursued if this is breached.

Disclaimer Notice:
Please note the information contained within this book is for motivational, educational and knowledge sharing purpose only. Every attempt has been made to provide the reader accurate, up to date and reliable complete information. No warranties of any kind are expressed or implied. Readers acknowledge that the author is not engaging in the rendering of legal, financial, medical or professional advice. By reading this document, the reader agrees that under no circumstances the author / publisher is responsible for any losses, direct or indirect, which are incurred as a result of the use of information contained within this document, including, but not limited to, —errors, omissions, or inaccuracies.

If you have further questions, contact on Tel: **+919969256731**
Email: **sandeepraviduttsharma@gmail.com**

Standing Tall
In Life

© Standing Tall In Life
BY SANDEEP RAVIDUTT SHARMA

Chase your dreams not just to fulfill them but also to see the next.

© Standing Tall In Life
BY SANDEEP RAVIDUTT SHARMA

Breakthroughs happen only when someone is pursuing and is determined to find the solution.

© Standing Tall In Life
BY SANDEEP RAVIDUTT SHARMA

Roses and Thorns grow together, but people choose the former. Everyone wants happiness in life but pain and suffering comes along either before or after. Be ready to face them all.

Keep an eye on your priorities and shuffle them with change in current circumstances. And you can win.

Don't get upset over your critics as lot of efforts goes even in finding faults of others.

Derive satisfaction with your deeds and not just by your dreams.

Why run to meet happiness when you have already heard its knock from within.

© Standing Tall In Life
BY SANDEEP RAVIDUTT SHARMA

You can't open the door locked from inside. First look within your mind and try to find the key of success and happiness.

Accept contradictions of life. Things or people who created storm yesterday are now your partners.

© **Standing Tall In Life**
BY SANDEEP RAVIDUTT SHARMA

Great people are those who inspire the world but still seek inspiration practicing humbleness.

Sometimes your words are enough to motivate others and make them feel wanted.

You can write stories of success with a positive mind.

Your mannerism speaks a lot about your bringing.

Wonderful are the ways of the Lord. He gives you the thought to buy a gift for someone and also helps you to package it with your unseen love.

| © **Standing Tall In Life** |
| BY SANDEEP RAVIDUTT SHARMA |

Write your story with your own thoughts and actions.

Nothing can stand in your way if you are determined and racing ahead.

Not everyone understands the pain of the other. Those who do should give their best to lift such souls.

Never ending arguments of hatred can only end with the single hug of love.

Learning comes from curiosity and interest.

Be the reason for someone to smile.

Marry hope with brilliant effort to give birth to Success.

© Standing Tall In Life
BY SANDEEP RAVIDUTT SHARMA

See your dreams taking shape through the mirror of efforts.

Move your eyes and not your mind while reading facts.

Never force other to walk in your shoes even when it fits their size.

© **Standing Tall In Life**
BY SANDEEP RAVIDUTT SHARMA

Strive to find purpose of your life and live with it further.

Decisions which you could not take in time keeps following you to tease. Use your knowledge to decide in time.

Don't expect best behaviour from someone wearing the best dress.

© **Standing Tall In Life**
BY SANDEEP RAVIDUTT SHARMA

Pearls of wisdom can be found on the Ocean bed of knowledge only by those who dare to dive. Be ready to take the first step and destination keeps coming closer.

Don't read script of your life but write it with your handful of efforts. God makes the way for those who take the first step forward.

System which doesn't value creativity that exist should be ignored. Creativity needs encouragement and patience.

While facing sea of challenges, keep rowing the boat of life with Oars of Patience and hope.

Hold on to your positive thoughts and let the discouraging ones leave before you. The positive thoughts have got the power to weave the world of togetherness and tranquility.

Answers point to the path where your curiosity can meet knowledge.

Flowers are ready to greet 'Good Morning' to you before you even begin your walk. Sunlight adds to their charm and makes them Smile.

Wonderful behaviour makes one look amazing.

Be led by your good thoughts instead of not so good life experiences. Good thoughts have got the power to create good life experiences.

Meet Hate if required with the handshake of Love.

Don't let your request sound like an order, just add please and I'm sure you will be delighted soon with the response from the other end.

Positive interaction is a two-way process. At least you can guarantee one end.

Think again about your aim if you have decided to take a risk. Without taking a risk all your thoughts remain thoughts forever. Innovation demands taking risk and exploring the unknown.

Nobody can really understand what you are going through. Be brave enough to face the storm.

Don't belittle someone's efforts however small it may be. Encourage others to give their best.

With your dedicated efforts let your idea of today become the tools and innovation of tomorrow.

Wake up to experience the rain of happiness.

Fight back to bring back Smile on your face.

Don't loose your patience when you are about to win. Many a times, the distance between the winner and loser is just a thin line of time, effort and patience.

The future holds a lot of possibilities while your present holds the power to shape these.

Blessings of the Lord are always with you. You just experience it more during your win. If you remember him during your period of pain and sufferings, you will much stronger to face them headon.

© Standing Tall In Life
BY SANDEEP RAVIDUTT SHARMA

Live your life today instead of accumulating too much for the future.

The ocean of joy also comes in a drop of tears.

Good intentions don't need too much of convincing.

Go with the flow only when all your attempts to divert the flow don't work.

© **Standing Tall In Life**
BY SANDEEP RAVIDUTT SHARMA

If your train doesn't come on time, you don't have to run for your destination. Just keep patience.

Keep your mind open to welcome all kinds of possibilities.

© Standing Tall In Life
BY SANDEEP RAVIDUTT SHARMA

Find ways to self motivate in order to stay positive.

Standing Tall In Life
BY SANDEEP RAVIDUTT SHARMA

Ambitions are good till the time it allows you to Live Now.

Standing Tall In Life
BY SANDEEP RAVIDUTT SHARMA

Escape from the clutches of ego and humility makes you happy.

Your strong visualisation has the power to attract things and people exactly as your mind portrays it.

Share your world with others, and it can turn into a wonderful Universe.

Don't pretend to agree unless you have really understood what is expected of you.

It's better to reconcile your differences with others rather than causing heartburn.

Each Sunrise paints the glow of positivity and brings cloud of happiness.

Don't spend your lifetime in making grand plans, find time to execute them.

The relationship thrives only on two way commitments. Without commitment it is just an arrangement.

Give priority to the important task and not the urgent ones.

Only those who woke up in time are fortunate enough to see the Sun rise.

Confidence comes from self-belief and knowledge.

Instead of choosing to disconnect from the world, it's better to make attempt and learn how to connect.

See left or right but walk straight in life.

Our prayers are always answered when purity of thought prevails and benefit of mankind dominates your mind.

Don't judge others based on your assumption of their thoughts about you.

You need to rise every day to face challenges and win.

The bundle of surprise awaits you when you least expect it.

You never know when your can help someone to discover their hidden talent.

To kick-start a good habit, you need to have a strong resolve.

Demand privileges only when you have delivered what was promised.

© Standing Tall In Life
BY SANDEEP RAVIDUTT SHARMA

Sometimes going for a long drive helps to develop good understanding.

Give your opinion but don't force it. Opinion becomes a rule when all concerned accepts it with open mind.

© Standing Tall In Life
BY SANDEEP RAVIDUTT SHARMA

You no longer need recommendation when people start giving your reference.

Define your goals, and it can motivate you to achieve them in time. Goals keep you engaged in activities that helps you to grow in life. Life with goals can take you to place of your choice rather than going nowhere.

You can afford the slide of your popularity but never ever your character.

You become a foreigner in your own country when you lose connection with the people on the ground.

Our priorities keep changing with passage of time. Accept change gracefully and move with time.

It's never too late to start learning newer things.

It's your confidence that helps you to find newer ways when you face dead end in your life path.

Let your Smile speak the language of humanity.

You can't stop obstacles coming your way but with positive thinking can very well choose another way.

You need complete focus and plan of action to realise your full potential.

Wonderful are the ways of the Lord, he makes one beg but stands with a bowl to feed at the very next door.

Expression in words hardly waits for grammatically correct language.

© **Standing Tall In Life**
BY SANDEEP RAVIDUTT SHARMA

Achieve your dreams while you are awake.

Let your setback become your motivation to try again and win this time.

It's your attitude towards life which makes all the difference.

Change your routine for the good and you start churning out the best.

Never abandon faith and trust till you have really tested it.

Knowing the future can influence your present only when you allow doing it.

© Standing Tall In Life
BY SANDEEP RAVIDUTT SHARMA

You gain experience when you lose a competition.

If failure made you Smile, it means you have learnt from your mistake.

Think about what you want in life instead of thinking the reverse.

Nothing is something which we don't know but are curious to explore. Keep Going, and you will get answers to all your questions.

www.ingramcontent.com/pod-product-compliance
Lightning Source LLC
Chambersburg PA
CBHW020545220526
45463CB00006B/2194